The Promise

A Citizen's Oath to America

Liam Sean

www.liamsean.com

The Promise/Liam Sean. -- 1st ed.
ISBN: 978-1-7349201-5-4

Cover design by Liam Sean

Cover art by Liam Sean

The Promise

A Citizen's Oath to America

Liam Sean

Works by Liam Sean

Fiction
Donald's Inferno
Wiley O' Wary

Non-Fiction
Uncommon Sense
The Promise

Screenplays
Ameriking
with Paul Lamb

Stage plays
Deathbed: A Comedy
with Dean Wilson

*To all those striving
for a more perfect
Union*

The Promise

A Citizen's Oath to America

I hereby swear to uphold and defend the Constitution of the United States of America.

I pledge to understand that this is a living document designed to evolve and mature as America strives to become a more perfect union.

As I yearn to be free, I fully acknowledge the same aspiration of my fellow Americans, and the huddled masses who dream to be Americans.

I vow to respect the human rights of all human beings.

I hold these truths to be self-evident: that all humans are created equal, that they are endowed by their creator with certain unalienable Rights, that among these are Life, Liberty and the Pursuit of Happiness.

As I breathe, I will foster peace and solidarity.

I solemnly do so of my own free will.

Chapter One

The Promise

America. The dream. The idea. The freedom. The promise it holds, and the promise we make to America itself.

From many, one. Many, as in *all* of us; one, as in *together*. One nation, indivisible. Each of us is the firewall to keep this nation undivided. Each of us, while yearning to be free, also shines the light of liberty for our fellow citizens and citizens to be.

A promise is a declaration or assurance that one will do a particular thing or that a particular thing will happen. It is a pledge, a vow, a guarantee. It is one's word of honor, an oath, a bond. It is a commitment, a contract, a covenant.

As Americans, the promise we make to ourselves, to each other, to our community and to the Nation itself, is the cornerstone of the Shining City on the Hill.

'And she's still a beacon, still a magnet for all who must have freedom, for all the pilgrims from all the lost places who are hurtling through the darkness, toward home.'

-Ronald Reagan

The greatness of America is in *its* promise to us. In the hope that freedom provides. In the ability to dream and be able to work toward those dreams.

The greatness of America is in its people. From many, One. From one, much.

The greatness of America is in its future. A future in which a more Perfect Union becomes more of a reality.

'What is that American promise? It's a promise that says each of us has the freedom to make of our lives what we will, but that we also have obligations to treat each other with dignity and respect.

'That's the promise of America, the idea that we are responsible for ourselves, but we also rise and fall as one nation, the fundamental belief that I am my brother's keeper, I am my sister's keeper.'

-Barack Obama

'America is a tune. It must be sung together.' -Gerald Stanley Lee

'America's a family. We all yell at each other. It all works out.'

-Louis C. K.

Chapter Two

Allegiance

'All who swear the oath of citizenship are doing more than completing a legal process. You are making a lifetime pledge to support the values and laws of America. The pledge comes with great privileges. It also comes with great responsibilities.'

-George W. Bush

As citizens of America, we are the threads that weave this most beautiful tapestry. An existing, breathing, working, playing, hoping, daring, failing and achieving, laughing, screaming, singing, shushing, dancing, distracting, confounding and infuriating work of art that is painfully and wonderfully alive. Each of us is indispensable. Each of us is necessary. We are each of us here by great fortune and by sheer struggle, and poetically, at a most important time in America's history.

And we are here to make a difference.

'Now, each of us must hold high the torch of citizenship in our lives. None of us can finish the race alone. We can only achieve our destiny together, one hand, one generation, one American connecting to another.'

-Bill Clinton

Next to the promise we make to our spouse, the promise we make to our children, next to that most sacred pact we make to be true to ourselves, the most important promise we make is to our country.

'In a few days I will lay down my official responsibilities in this office, to take up once more the only title in our democracy superior to that of President, the title of citizen.'

-Jimmy Carter

The Naturalization Oath of Allegiance asks firstly to renounce any allegiance to a foreign power. It then asks the future citizen to support the Constitution, and if necessary, to defend the Constitution. It requires the speaker to bear true faith and allegiance to the Constitution, and that this Oath was made of their own free will.

For citizens who were born here, this Oath is missing. It is assumed, presumed, expected. Indeed, it is quite another thing to stand in a room filled with people, to raise your right hand and swear an Oath. Even staring oneself in the eyes before a mirror, right hand held up, words memorized, holds more meaning than an implied expectation. And that may be where some slippage can occur. Because there is privilege in this assumption. A degree of privilege that reaps the rewards without imparting the work that is requested. And as we all know, to whom much is given, much is required.

'You are a citizen, and citizenship carries responsibilities.'

-Paul Collier

'Citizenship is an attitude, a state of mind, an emotional conviction that the whole is greater than the part.'

-Robert A. Heinlein

'Citizens by birth or choice, of a common country, that country has a right to concentrate your affections.'

'The name of American, which belongs to you, in your national capacity, must always exalt the just pride of Patriotism.'

'It is incumbent on every person of every description to contribute to his country's welfare.'

-George Washington

Chapter Three

One Fine Idea

I hereby swear to uphold and defend the Constitution of the United States of America.

'Ours is the only country deliberately founded on a good idea.'

-John Gunther

A nation founded on an idea must work to uphold that idea. Unlike any other form of government before America, the focal point of our Nation, of our unity, is nebulous, hard to hold. Easily lost. Easily stolen.

'The price of Liberty is eternal vigilance.'

-John Philpot Curran

Vigilance starts here. By affirming our intent, by promising to our country, our community, to each other and to ourselves, that the incredible, light-affirming idea of the American Constitution is something worth believing in. Worth living by. Worth defending.

'Tyranny, like hell, is not easily conquered, yet, we have this consolation with us, that the harder the conflict, the more glorious the triumph.'

-Thomas Paine

We are a nation built on laws. Laws created by humans, generation after generation. These laws are not perfect. As the nation evolves and grows, these laws become more refined. Some are repealed. Others rise as newer situations and modernity create the need for new laws. It isn't a perfect science. It is wholly and wonderfully messy and human. But it comes, in essence, from all of us, for all of us.

These laws are the primary and most civil way to defend the Constitution and the freedoms that lie within its words. Every day, as a people, we live by these laws. We practice them. They protect us and uphold our way of life. This is why we swear an oath to the Constitution. Without this affirmation, there would be no structure. There would be no life, liberty, or pursuit of happiness. Without just laws, there would be no democracy.

'Democracy is not a state. It is an act, and each generation must do its part.'

-John Lewis

'Democracies are more than a form of government, they're a way of being, of seeing the world, a way that defines who we are, what we believe, why we do what we do. We must, in this moment, dig deep within ourselves and recognize that we can't take democracy for granted any longer.'

-Joe Biden

Chapter Four

It Is Alive!

I pledge to understand that this is a living document designed to evolve and mature as America strives to become a more perfect union.

'Our Founders said we're giving you a Republic, if you can keep it, and they also said, we have a

Constitution and we're going to form a more perfect union.'

-Barbara Boxer

This Promise runs deep. We have pledged all of ourselves, body, soul and heart, to life, liberty and happiness. We have embraced the most significant phrase in human history, *that all people are created equal*, and in doing so have sworn to uphold the document that serves as the touchstone for all we hold dear.

We have also agreed to the principle that this is a Living

Document, meant to change, evolve and mature as the times surrounding the Nation likewise change and evolve.

'I confess that there are several parts of this Constitution which I do not at present approve, but I am not sure I shall never approve them. For having lived long, I have experienced many instances of being obliged by better information, or fuller consideration, to change opinions even on important subjects, which I once thought right, but found to be otherwise.'

-Benjamin Franklin

In 1789, the year the Constitution was written, America was far from being a Perfect Union. Roughly half the population of nearly four million people were allowed to vote. 700,000 human beings were enslaved, women had few rights at all, and a centuries-long campaign to disenfranchise and eliminate the Indigenous Americans was well under way.

When we look at these facts with a perception and level of humanity that has evolved and matured, we understand how heinous these exceptions are to *'All Men Being Created Equal.'* This is the single largest piece of evidence in recognizing the Constitution as being a Living Document.

'Laws and institutions must go hand in hand with the progress of the human mind. As that becomes more developed, more enlightened, as new discoveries are made, new truths disclosed, and manners and opinions change with the change of circumstances, institutions must advance also, and keep pace with the times. We might as well require a man to wear still the coat which fitted him when a boy, as civilized society to remain ever under the regimen of their barbarous ancestors.'

-Thomas Jefferson

The wording of the Constitution can be infuriatingly vague. Generations of lawmakers have beseeched the Founding Fathers for a bit more clarity in each phrase, each amendment. This is the second piece of evidence that the Constitution is a touchstone, not a sacred relic etched in stone. To hold every word up as too hallowed to be yielding is either complete folly, or an attempt to exploit the original text. Many an American political faction has, and is, using the Constitution's ambiguity for political gain. And that's where we all come in, to understand, uphold and defend. Particularly, when one or several of the branches of our own government fails to serve the people.

'The strength of the Constitution lies entirely in the determination of each citizen to defend it. Only if every single citizen feels duty bound to do his share in this defense are the constitutional rights secure.'

-Albert Einstein

'However the Court may interpret the provisions of the Constitution, it is still the Constitution which is the law and not the decision of the Court.'

-Charles Warren

'The writers of the U.S. Constitution used "a more perfect union" to express their goal of establishing a country with a system of government as close to ideal as possible engaged in a continuous cycle of improvement.'

-Patrick Capriola

So, just what is this '*Perfect Union*?' The answer is in the preamble of the Constitution, where six goals are laid out in those most revolutionary words.

To form a more perfect union: to organize a stronger government to maintain law and order, but weak enough to not restrict liberty.

To establish justice: to ensure fairness and equality for all citizens.

To ensure domestic tranquility: to keep peace and order within the nation.

To provide for the common defense: to protect the nation from enemies and threats.

To promote the general welfare: to support the well-being and happiness of all the people.

To secure the Blessings of Liberty for ourselves and our posterity: to safeguard the inherent rights of Life, Liberty and the Pursuit of Happiness for those living today and those who will follow.

The success of these goals centers on understanding that *All Humans Are Created Equal* and that each of those humans has basic, fundamental rights.

'All men were made by the same Great Spirit Chief. They are brothers. The Earth is the Mother of all people, and all the people should have equal rights to live upon it.'

-Chief Joseph

'Men talk of the Negro problem; there is no Negro problem. The problem is whether American people have loyalty enough, honor enough, patriotism enough, to live up to their own Constitution.'

-Frederick Douglass

'The true republic: men, their rights and nothing more; women, their rights and nothing less.'

-Susan B. Anthony

'Once social change begins, it cannot be reversed. You cannot un-educate the person who has learned to read. You cannot humiliate the person who feels pride. You cannot oppress the people who are not afraid anymore.'

-Cesar Chavez

Perfection is an impossible and frustrating destination. The journey is the reward, and that journey is a nation that strives for excellence, acceptance, equality, equity and unity. In the words of Benjamin Franklin, we must all hang together, or assuredly we shall all hang separately.

'Then join hand in hand, brave Americans all! By uniting we stand, by dividing we fall!'

-John Dickinson

Chapter Five

My Heart's Home

As I yearn to be free, I fully acknowledge the same aspiration of my fellow Americans, and the huddled masses who dream to be Americans.

'Oh, it's home again and home again, America for me! I want a ship that's westward bound to plough the rolling sea, To the blessed land of Room Enough beyond the ocean bars, Where the air is full of sunlight and the flag is full of stars.'

-Henry Van Dyke

Like the very breath of life itself, each human being yearns to be free. It is innate. Fundamental. Coded. It is as if our hearts were fife and drum, the cadence of the music calling us to liberty.

Human history has been driven by this need to be free, the essential ideals of which are embodied in the Constitution. Beginning with these words, *We the People*, the course of human destiny became inextricably woven with liberty and justice for all. This is, and always has been, a work in progress. But what great work it is!

'America represents something universal in the human spirit. Anybody from any corner of the world can come to America to live and become an American.'

-Ronald Reagan.

The first task in the daily work of practicing freedom is to acknowledge the freedom of every other American. We must do so even to those who are in competition against us, whose views and values seem radically different than our own, even to those who do not seem to be living up to their share of the *Promise*. Defeat lies in judgement; victory begins with respect.

'To be true to one's own freedom is, in essence, to honor and respect the freedom of all others.'

-Dwight D. Eisenhower

This is no easy task. Also coded deep within us are algorithms based on survival, on instincts rooted in fear, in hunger, in the drive to reproduce copies of ourselves. As civilization rose up from these base instincts, humans have attained higher values. Among these are compassion, empathy, and cooperation, intellect, growth and self-worth, freedom, fairness and purpose. As civilizations rose, it was inevitable that these words would finally be written: *All People Are Created Equal*. In that single sentence, human beings were tasked with rising above the base instincts and moving forward together.

Life, Liberty and the Pursuit of Happiness are the inalienable rights of all human beings. All aspirations, hopes and dreams come from those rights. And America, as imperfect as she has been, is the beacon for these freedoms.

'Once I thought to write a history of the immigrants in America. Then I discovered that the immigrants were American history.'

-Oscar Handlin

'We become not a melting pot but a beautiful mosaic. Different people, different beliefs, different yearnings, different hopes, different dreams.'

-Jimmy Carter

'The bosom of America is open to receive not only the Opulent and respected Stranger, but the oppressed and persecuted of all Nations and Religions; whom we shall welcome to a participation of all our rights and privileges.

-George Washington

'I had always hoped that this land might become a safe and agreeable asylum to the virtuous and persecuted part of mankind, to whatever nation they might belong.'

-George Washington

'People come here penniless but not cultureless. They bring us gifts. We can synthesize the best of our traditions with the best of theirs. We can teach and learn from each other to produce a better America.'

-Mary Pipher

Chapter Six

Better Angels

I vow to respect the human rights of all human beings.

'We shall overcome because the arc of the moral universe is long, but it bends toward justice.'

-Martin Luther King

Life, Liberty and the Pursuit of Happiness doesn't happen without understanding that all humans have these inalienable rights. Which, in itself, doesn't happen without recognizing, respecting, and if need be, defending the fundamental human rights of each of us.

Government governs by the consent of the governed to protect these fundamental rights. The Constitution protects these rights as the cornerstone law of the land. It is the prism through which all laws are founded.

The Constitution is not, nor was ever meant to be, etched in stone. An immovable, unchangeable sacred relic. What is sacred are the human rights that it protects, and all law should be based first and foremost on protecting human rights. Property and profit are a distant second and third to human rights.

'The care of human life and happiness, and not their destruction, is the first and only object of good government.'

-Benjamin Franklin

'Government is instituted for the common good; for the protection, safety, prosperity, and happiness of the people; and not for the profit, honor, or private interest of any one man, family, or class of men.'

-John Adams

'The purpose of government is to enable the people of a nation to live in safety and happiness. Government exists for the interests of the governed, not for the governors.'

-Thomas Jefferson

The 'governors' include that oligarchy of monied industrialists who have and still try, to pervert the Constitution for their own profit. It has been through the persistent, rebellious, righteous will of the American people to rise-up and smack that oligarchy back in place, that human rights have been defended.

'We the people are the rightful masters of both Congress and the courts, not to overthrow the

Constitution, but to overthrow the men who pervert the Constitution.'

-Abraham Lincoln

The vow we make to respect each other's human rights is as innate a part of ourselves as the need for friendship, the want to be loved and accepted. It is wholly a part of us. It is that wonderful American love for the underdog, the want to see people succeed and not to suffer. That desire to offer a hand-up, to help-out, to work together. It is a core value that is enshrined in the spirit of this nation. Hope, faith and charity are fundamental values that sing every bit as loud as patriotism and reach much deeper notes. And each of us can carry that tune.

'We are not enemies, but friends. We must not be enemies. Though passion may have strained it must not break our bonds of affection. The mystic chords of memory, stretching from every battlefield and patriot grave to every living heart and hearthstone all over this broad land, will yet swell the chorus of the Union, when again touched, as surely they will be, by the better angels of our nature.'

-Abraham Lincoln

In a society so dominated by material excess, it becomes all too easy to forget humans. In a society in which humans are increasingly isolated by social media, it is equally easy to not see the human in the human being we are engaging with. Those primary precepts of simplicity, patience and compassion can be easily bowled over by complexity, callousness and cruelty.

In understanding the *Promise*, we have pledged to ourselves to recognize the human being and the American in our fellow citizens. To have the patience to empathize with them and likewise to have compassion for whatever it is they are going through. It is in this simple way that we build respect and dignity, the cornerstones of human rights.

Unity begins here.

'Together, all things are possible.'

-Cesar Chavez

Chapter Seven

Truth

I hold these truths to be self-evident: that all humans are created equal, that they are endowed by their creator with certain unalienable Rights, that among these are Life, Liberty and the Pursuit of Happiness.

We stand together. United by these words. United in knowing we have more in common than what is different. United in the desire to live our lives as we each see fit, guided by an inner compass that yearns to be free.

Life. Liberty. Happiness. In a word: love.

'Let us work together for unity and love.'

-Mahatma Gandhi

'Love creates an "us" without destroying the "me".'

-Leo Buscaglia

'Love conquers all. Love is the grace that transcends any kind of injustice in the end.'

-Mark Ruffalo

Deep within us is an interconnectedness to all beings on this planet, and at a more profound frequency, every other human. Like the pure sound of a bell ringing, the

Truths in the Constitution our deepest self recognizes.

We are all created equal. Each of us has the right to be free, to live a life of our choosing, and to do so without fear.

And happiness. Happiness as the pursuit of virtue; happiness as *being* good, rather than feeling good. In the same way that the mycorrhizal network of fungus connects trees and allows trees to communicate with each other, at some deep, primordial level we are just as connected. That's why it feels so good to help. That's why it feels so good being good. This is why the *Beatitudes* are so beautiful and so powerful.

'Only a virtuous people are capable of freedom.'

-Benjamin Franklin

'The more he does for others, the more he has. The more he gives to others, the more he has.'

-Lao Tzu

The *Promise* we make to America hinges on this *esprit de corps*. That feeling of pride, fellowship and loyalty we get when we work together for a common community goal. When we stand and hear the National Anthem. When we watch our children in the park playing with other children they have never met before.

And there it is. That amazing ability of children to love and accept. That genuineness. That honesty. That love. That is the key.

'When you think like a child, your imagination is free and anything is possible.'

-Chris Angel

We quite literally make the world around us with every action or inaction. In living our lives in freedom and fellowship we allow every other American to do the same. As Nelson Mandella said, "As we let our own light shine, we unconsciously give other people permission to do the same."

The Constitution provides the framework, the touchstone, and the primary law to do all of this. It codifies that intrinsic human love of wanting to do the right thing, of wanting to come together. It creates the space for the pure joy of relishing the freedom of all those around us.

'Love life. Engage in it. Give it all you've got. Love it with a passion because life truly does give back, many times over, what you put into it.'

-Maya Angelou

We live and let live. And by doing so, are given the miracle of watching everyone around us thrive. We are afforded the opportunity to be a part of something bigger than ourselves, to be a part of something wonderful. All this while at the same time embracing our own success. The *Promise* we make to ourselves, each other, America, it is quite literally the catalyst for all of this to happen. The energy in this is exponential. The power behind it is love. And freedom? Freedom makes it possible.

'Have enough courage to trust love one more time and always one more time.'

-Maya Angelou

Chapter Eight

Gather Together

As I breathe, I will foster peace and solidarity.

'We rise by lifting others.'

-Unknown

    Without peace, there is no future. Without peace, there is no freedom. No liberty. No happiness. And therefore, no life.

'There is no peace without fairness, truth, justice and solidarity.'

-John Paul II

'The rights of every man are diminished when the rights of one man are threatened.'

-John F. Kennedy

   Peace begins in each of our hearts. It begins by understanding that each of us is paramount to the survival and success of us all. That understanding is founded on the basic principle that we are all created equal, that each of has intrinsic value, and that respect fosters love.

'Love is the cause of unity in all causes.'

-Aristotle

The kaleidoscope of diversity in America openly challenges every heart to acknowledge these fundamental concepts. It asks each of us to set aside prejudices and to accept each other as equals, as

Americans. This is the breath of life of this country.

'Our first teacher is our own heart.'

-Cheyenne proverb

There are those instances where we have come together as a nation. World War II. Two pandemics. The Great Depression. Nine-Eleven. Those times of national crisis where threatened and hurting, we rallied together.

Imagine.

Imagine if instead, the root cause of coming together was not to defend and survive, but to lift and achieve. To foster peace and solidarity. To truly be the Shining City on the Hill; the Light of Lady Liberty.

'We have it in our power to begin the world over again.'

-Thomas Paine

We wake up each morning not just with the promise of a new day, but with the promise of a new world. If the butterfly effect in Chaos Theory holds true, that small changes can make big differences, then the power of love, the purity of peace and the strength of solidarity are difference makers on a universal scale. All it takes is that intention: to love, to foster peace, to come together. All it takes is the commitment to build, unify and see all of us as one people, as one nation. Making a promise to believe and work towards a more perfect union, one task at a time, one community at a time, one relationship at a time.

'Never doubt that a small group of thoughtful, committed citizens can change the world; indeed, it's the only thing that ever has.'

-Margaret Mead

"Alone we can do so little; together we can do so much.'

-Hellen Keller

'What is the essence of life? To serve others and to do good.'

-Aristotle

Chapter Nine

Deep Sincerity

I solemnly do so of my own free will.

'I am not bound to win, but I am bound to be true. I am not bound to succeed, but I am bound to live up to what light I have.'

-Abraham Lincoln

This third stone from the Sun that we cling to is the only home we know. It is our everything. The narrow impossibility of life gets lost in the toils of every day living. Eight billion people call this planet home. Less than thirty percent of them live in a democracy.

Let's not mince words: there is only one type of government that allows freedom and that is a liberal democracy. A democratic system of government in which individual rights and freedoms are officially recognized and protected, and the exercise of political power is limited by the rule of law.

Democracy is as fragile as life itself. It takes a solemn oath of commitment, a concerted effort and a lot of heart to keep democracy alive.

'Lift every voice and sing till earth and heaven ring, ring with harmonies of liberty.'

-African American Anthem

We must keep faith in this commitment. The Constitution is the touchstone. Our life and the lives of our fellow citizens are all the incentive we need. The *Promise* we've made to ourselves, each other and to America, sets the tone and provides the direction. Failure in this is not an option. Quite simply, at this moment on the third stone from the Sun, all of life depends on democracy succeeding.

'Our obligations to our country never cease but with our lives. We ought to do all we can.'

-John Adams

'A nation, as a society, forms a moral person, and every member of it is personally responsible for his society.'

-Thomas Jefferson

Our free will is the power of *acting*. It is a noun with the power of a verb. It is the ability to act and make a difference; the incredible feat of taking control of your life and using that self-determination to be a part of society. It is through this action that we change the world: the world in ourselves and the world around us.

Love. Respect. Fostering peace and solidarity. Exercising democracy. These are all actions that begin by being true to ourselves, by sharing our light and by working together.

'Do all the good you can
By all the means you can,
In all the ways you can,
In all the places you can,
At all the times you can
To all the people you can,
As long as ever you can.'

-John Wesley

There is no greater testament to the solemn nature of taking an oath than those who have given their lives so others may be free. Americans who sacrificed everything to ensure that freedom would endure; that the Light of the Constitution and of Lady Liberty would shine on. From the battlefields of wars both just and unjust, from the marches to demand equal rights, to the workers' strikes in the face of violent oppression, citizens of all colors, creeds and genders have given their lives so others can live their dreams.

'Solidarity is based on the principle that we are willing to put ourselves at risk to protect each other.'

-Starhawk

'With great victory comes great sacrifice.'

-Theodore Roosevelt

We must always remember the sacrifices that have been made so we may be this fortunate. Those who made these sacrifices rightly demand of us the participation in

American democracy. It demands reverence, deep sincerity and respect for the sacrifices made and the issues at hand. There is a saying that when America sneezes, the world catches a cold. Our votes quite literally affect the lives of eight billion people. Our policies determine the well-being of all life on this planet.

'Never underestimate the influence you have on others.'

-Laurie Buchanan

'We can change the world and make it a better place. It is in our hands to make a difference.'

-Nelson Mandella

What makes this *Promise* so powerful is that it comes from our hearts. It emanates with a radiance of light and warmth like an inner sun. Three hundred and thirty million Americans has this inside of them. Three hundred and thirty million Americans linked together in an energy grid of resolve, of love, of forging a more perfect union.

There is no end to what we can accomplish.

'So powerful is the light of unity that it can illuminate the whole earth.'

-Bahà'u'llá

Chapter Ten

Touchstones

'We hold these truths to be self-evident, that all men are created equal, that they are endowed by their creator with certain unalienable rights, that among these are Life, Liberty and the Pursuit of Happiness.'

-The United States Declaration of Independence

'That to secure these rights, Governments are instituted among Men, deriving their just powers from the consent of the governed.'

-The United States Declaration of Independence

'The purpose of government is to enable the people of a nation to live in safety and happiness.'

-Thomas Jefferson

'As the happiness of the people is the sole end of government, so the consent of the people is the only foundation of it, in reason, morality, and the natural fitness of things.'

-John Adams

'The people are the only sure reliance for the preservation of liberty.'

-Thomas Jefferson

'The object of government is the welfare of the people. The material progress and prosperity of a nation are desirable chiefly so far as they lead to the moral and material welfare of all good citizens.'

-Teddy Roosevelt

'We must have the courage to do what we know is morally right.'

-Ronald Reagan

'The time is always right to do what is right.'

-Martin Luther King

'Not like the brazen giant of Greek fame,

With conquering limbs astride from land to land:

Here at our sea-washed, sunset gates shall stand

A mighty woman with a torch, whose flame is the imprisoned lightning, and her name,

Mother of Exiles. From her beacon-hand

Glows world-wide welcome; her mild eyes command

The air-bridged harbor that twin cities frame.

"Keep, ancient lands, your storied pomp!"

cries she

With silent lips. "Give me your tired, your poor,

Your huddled masses yearning to breathe free,

The wretched refuse of your teeming shore.

Send these, the homeless, the tempest-tossed to me,

I lift my lamp beside the golden door!"'

-Emma Lazarus

The poem on a bronze plaque inside the Statue of Liberty.

The Promise

A Citizen's Oath to America

I hereby swear to uphold and defend the Constitution of the United States of America.

I pledge to understand that this is a living document designed to evolve and mature as America strives to become a more perfect union.

As I yearn to be free, I fully acknowledge the same aspiration of my fellow Americans, and the huddled masses who dream to be Americans.

I vow to respect the human rights of all human beings.

I hold these truths to be self-evident: that all humans are created equal, that they are endowed by their creator with certain unalienable Rights, that among these are Life, Liberty and the Pursuit of Happiness.

As I breathe, I will foster peace and solidarity.

I solemnly do so of my own free will.

ABOUT THE AUTHOR

Liam Sean is a writer, musician, actor, graphic artist, and chef who dwells deep within the Boreal Forests of the Upper Great Lakes. For projects & info, please wander to www.liamsean.com